© 2013 Will Strange.

All rights reserved.

Published by Will Strange.

ISBN: 978-1-291-61908-9

An Architectural Model

Contents

Introduction **14**

What is this book for?   16

A note about laser cutting: 18

Parts of the model: 19

Key: 23

Design **26**

Basic principles: 28

Designing the model: 30

Why simplify?   32

Too small to model: 34

Unnecessary detail: 36

Deliberate simplification: 38

Preparation for making: 40

Baseboard **44**

The 'carcass':   46

'Cladding':   48

Pavements and surface detail: 50

Water: 52

'Site'	**54**
Basics:	56
CAD drawings 1:	58
CAD drawings 2:	62
Preparing elevations:	64
Assembling the walls:	66
Elevations:	68
Roof:	72
Roof windows:	74
Ridge tiles:	76
Masking:	77
Painting:	78
Summary:	80
Context 1	**82**
Good practice:	86
Simplest context buildings:	90
Basic roof profiles:	91
Planning ahead:	92
Assembly:	94

Simple barn buildings:	96
Bungalow:	98

Context 2 .... **100**

Cutting model-board blocks:	102
Roof shape:	104
Elevation detail:	106
Roof detail / texture:	108
Steps:	110
Chapel:	112
Cutting blocks for the chapel:	113
Chapel elevations:	114
Chapel assembly:	116
Chapel roof panels:	118
Cutting to fit the baseboard:	120

Context 3 .... **122**

Detailed context:	124
Model board blocks:	126
Facades and chimneys:	128

'Extension':   130
Door detail: 131
Cornice detail: 132
Open sided buildings: 136
Assembly: 138
'Casting' detail to fit: 140

Final Details **144**
Trees: 146
Twisting wire: 148
Finishing and 'planting':   151
Walls and fences: 156
Raised pools: 158
Pergola: 160

Reference **166**
Tools: 168
Sanding blocks: 172
MDF: 174
Plywood: 175

Acrylic:	176
Polystyrene sheet:	177
Textured polystyrene:	178
Model board:	179
P.V.A glue:	180
Solvent:	181
Contact adhesive:	182
'Superglue':	183
Polyester filler:	184

Introduction

Many books are available that describe the use of scale models in 'getting to' the design of buildings and structures. Many offer insight into the history, meaning and importance of the act of modelmaking.

It is the aim of this book to do neither of those and instead to offer a description of the techniques employed by professional modelmakers in the making of a great many

commercial models that are commissioned regularly.

Models for exhibitions, trade fairs, public consultation and marketing make up the 'bread and butter' of the professional architectural modelmaking industry.

These are often not 'glamorous' or 'artistic' objects, but they serve their purpose well and offer an interesting technical challenge to their makers.

What is this book for?

It is the intension of this book to illustrate and raise awareness of *some* of the principles, materials and techniques that are employed by professional modelmakers. It may, therefore, be necessary to adapt the principles illustrated here for other models.

One of the most valuable skills of the professional modelmaker is the ability to adapt materials, techniques and processes to fit any given model that they are called upon to make.

The buildings that feature in this book are rather generic and the location of the proposed site is deliberately left ambiguous. It is intended that this could be a model of a development anywhere, in the hope that this will help the to descriptions be adapted for other contexts.

Some of the building details are therefore simplified, representing a chance to demonstrate a variety of modeling techniques rather than an accurate depiction of a real location.

A note about Laser Cutting:

The laser cutter has become an everyday piece of machinery for most architectural modelmakers, taking its place alongside the more traditional table saw, bandsaw and circular sander.

The techniques of laser cutting acrylic sheet and combining it block and sheet material fashioned by more traditional means are therefore deliberately employed here to properly represent contemporary practice.

This is not a step by step guide for anyone to be able to follow, but rather a description and

illustration of some of the techniques that need to be mastered to work as a professional architectural modelmaker today.

Parts of the model:

The following chapters represent a common way to divide the parts that need to be made and brought
        together

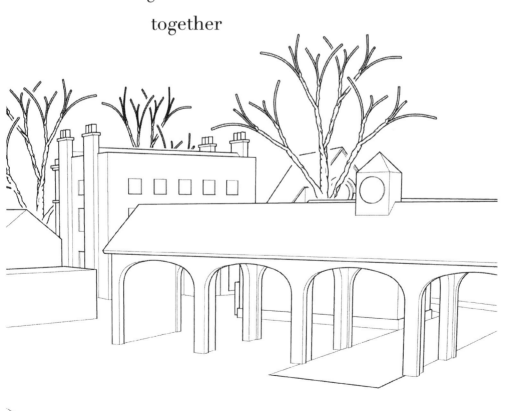

to create a model.

'Site' describes the proposal or new building that is the subject of the model and the focus for a designer and the audience.

The 'baseboard' is the box that holds other parts together and represents the land and road / path layout.

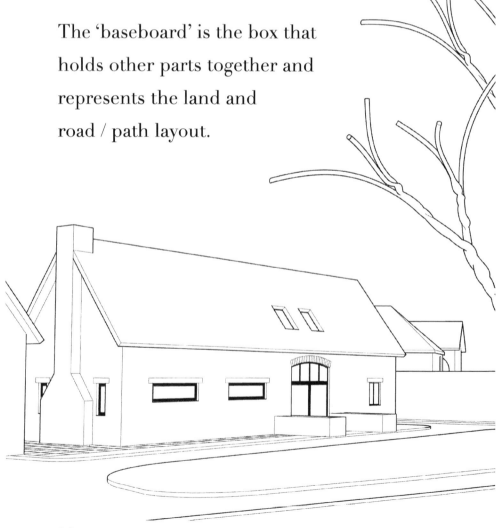

'Context' usually refers to all that is not site or baseboard. The buildings that surround the

site, but are not changed by any new proposals. This detail helps to explain how something that is yet to be built will fit into an area by showing familiar landmarks.

'Details' are the fine detail on site, baseboard and context that are added at the final stage of making the model. These are usually made as small 'sub-assemblies' that can be assembled and painted separately.

A 'reference' section is included to give a little more detail about some materials, adhesives and processes that are used in the architectural modeling industry, and throughout the book. This section is not exhaustive, concentrating on techniques that are referred to in this book, and should be read as part of a wider 'diet' of research.

Key:

Throughout this book a series of diagrams and symbols are used to describe the processes, adhesives and materials that are used in the construction of the model. A key to these is shown here and further description is included in the reference chapter, along with other 'general knowledge' about modelmaking practice.

After materials are introduced and processes become more complex, fewer symbols are used, details being given in the text.

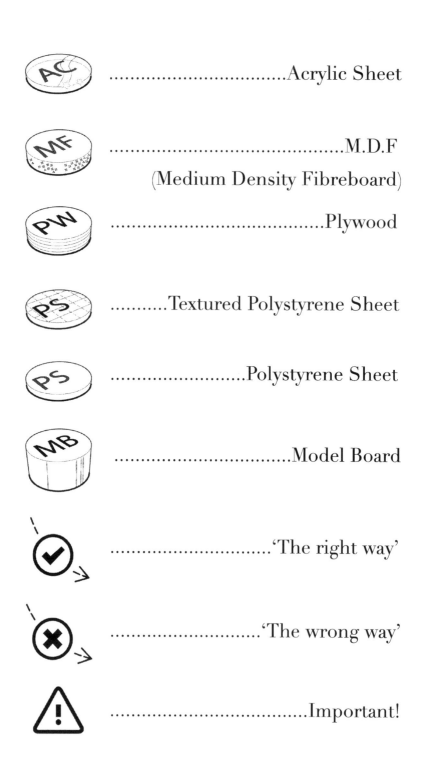

P.V.A..
(Wood Glue)

Solvent..

Contact Adhesive............................

Cyanoacrylate / CA glue.................
(Super-Glue)

Body Filler......................................

Acrylic Paint...................................

Masking Tape.................................

Allow time to dry / set....................

Design

Basic principles:

Some basic principles apply to most kinds of architectural model. The example featured in this book is a very simple one but demonstrates many of the 'conventions' that are used by architectural modelmakers.

The shape and extent of the baseboard is designed to ensure that all of the important parts of the 'site' and 'context' can be included on the 'base'. In this instance, the shape of the baseboard is such that a chapel is included at one corner (a local landmark, helping to show the location of the model) and barn buildings (that have influenced the style of the 'site') are included at the edges.

Many of the components are cut from flat sheet material and then assembled to make more complicated shapes. Despite the potential for rapid prototyping to enable the modelmaker to print whole models in one operation, a great many commercial architectural models are still made with techniques that are well established. Rapid prototyping techniques would make it easier to create more organic or irregular forms. In this case the style of the architecture lends itself to being assembled from flat components.

Materials are chosen for their suitability to make the model as quickly and efficiently as possible. Acrylic sheet is easy to cut accurately with a laser cutter, so is chosen for parts that need to be accurate and / or have lots of detail laser etched into them. Polystyrene sheet is much cheaper, but cannot be easily cut with a laser. Pavement pads are made with polystyrene though, as these can be cut accurately *enough* with a scalpel, perhaps by laying a copy of the site plan drawing onto the material and cutting through it.

The need to design the model:

Though a scale model is made from drawings that describe a real building, the *model* must still be *designed* by the modelmaker.

The designer / architect will design a building, not a model. It is the job of the modelmaker to design something that looks like a 'real' proposal, but has a very different use and is made in a very different way. In this way the model should be seen as a new object in its own right, albeit one that, superficially, looks like another.

Any model is usually simplified a great deal compared with reality. The degree to which it is simplified will depend on what the model is designed to show, the size that details reduce to at scale and the time available to make the model.

It is this simplification that necessitates the design input of the modelmaker.

Why simplify?

There are three main reasons for simplification of the model compared to the 'real' design...

- Detail is too small, at the scale of the model, to reasonably make. At different scales the same design may be represented quite differently, as a larger scale model can be made more 'accurately'. Often, small details are possible to make, but omitted because to do so would be too time consuming (and therefore expensive).

- There is no need to show a detail. Interior detail, for instance, will often not be seen so it's omitted. Sometimes, decisions about whether detail should be modeled or not will be taken with the available budget in mind. Including more detail will take more time, which will increase the necessary cost of making the model.

- Detail is deliberately simplified to imply that a part of the model has less value or status than another. All context buildings are simplified to some degree. The style of the model can make a big difference to how the model is 'read'. Different levels of detail are often used to suggest a hierarchy for the elements of the model, some parts being given more importance than others.

Too small to model?

The cornice detail of a detailed context building is an example of this kind of simplification.

Modeled in complete accuracy (using the techniques described in a later chapter) some of the pieces of polystyrene would need to be so small as to be very difficult to handle.

The detail is represented by strips that can give the right 'style' of shape. close enough to reality to capture the character of the building.

Modeled in complete accuracy, at a small scale, the model would likely not appear any more accurate since all of the other details in the building have been simplified too.

The overall height of the cornice detail is still correct. Only the level of detail is reduced.

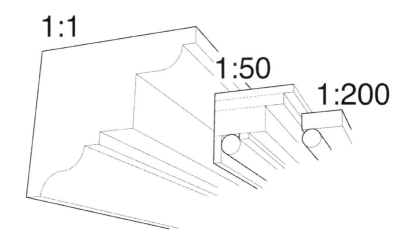

Tip: When deciding how much to simplify a building when modeling it as 'context', imagine the amount of detail that would be visible if looking down on it from a distance. At distance we recognise objects by their outlines and massing, not by their fine detail and texture.

Unnecessary detail:

It is not feasible to make a model by simply building it in the same way that a real building is made. Since only the detail on the outside of the building would be visible in this model, that is all that is modeled.

Architectural models are *representations* of their subjects, never *replicas*.

A section of the 'site' serves as an example of the way that the model is simplified. In the 'real' section walls have 2 skins and a cavity with insulation, the roof consists of timber beams and individual tiles and the whole building sits on foundations dug in to the ground below what can be seen.

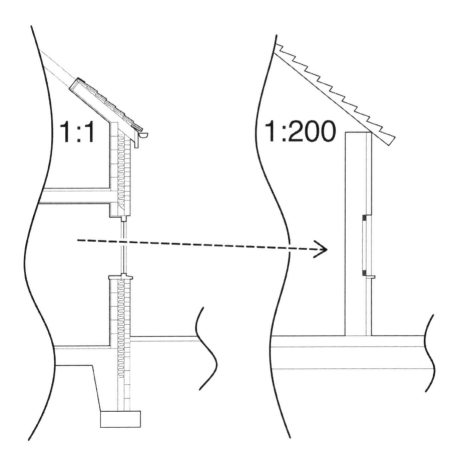

The model reduces these details to just 2 layers of acrylic sheet, a single thickness of textured polystyrene sheet and the building is 'cut' at ground level to sit on the flat surface of the baseboard.

Tip: At larger scales another layer might be added to give 'depth' to the window frames. This will be more realistic since in reality the frame sits proud of the glass.

Deliberate simplification:

As a general rule, the further 'context' is from the 'site', the less detail will be included.

The simplest blocks, that represent barns in this book's example, show the minimum level of detail that might usually be included.

- The overhang of the roof at the eaves is not modeled at all.
- Wall and roof texture is modeled smooth.
- No attempt is made to represent windows or doors (or the apertures for them).
- The 'plinth' detail around the base is omitted.

While these models are simple compared to reality important details are still correct...

- The overall size and shape of the building, in plan, is correct.
- The heights of the blocks are correct at the ridge and eaves of the roof.
- The pitch of the roof is correct.
- The relationship between the buildings, distance from kerb edges etc. are correct.

Preparation for making the model:

Before anything for the model is made, a set of drawings is needed. Without full knowledge of what will be built it is impossible to plan for all of the pieces of the model that will need to fit together later.

Plans, sections and elevations are needed to fully understand
what is to be made.
Often these
will be

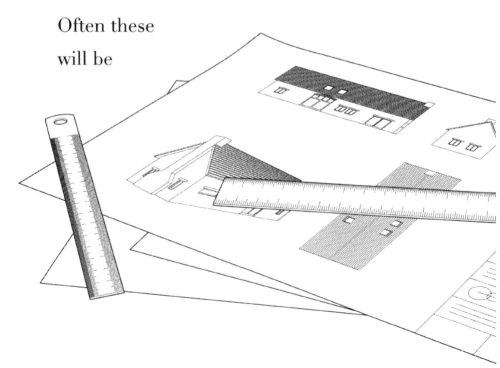

provided to the modelmaker in a form that is designed for making the 'real' proposal.

The modelmaker will often then recreate, or at least re-scale, these drawings so that they represent the scale model instead.

In order to cut parts of the model with a laser cutter, 'cleaner' drawings will be needed than might be produced for constructing the real building. These will be simpler than those drawn for construction as they will only

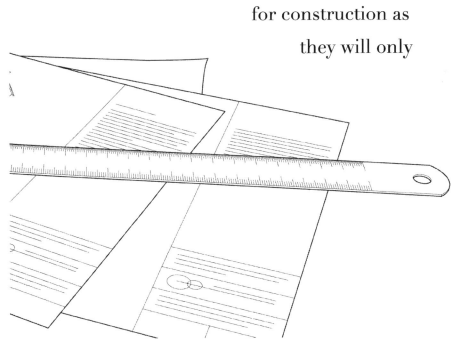

include the lines that need to be cut and etched.

The swimming pool, next to the 'site' building, serves as an example of this forward planning. In order to allow a block of acrylic to be set into the baseboard at the right height to represent the water, a hole must be cut through the baseboard.

This is easiest to do while the baseboard is being made.

Tip: More complicated baseboards, with contoured surfaces, will need very careful planning to enable 'context' and 'site' buildings to be set into the landscape during the final assembly of the model.

Tip: Drawings should be printed at the scale that the model will be made, especially the plan of the whole site. This will enable measurements to be taken and compared easily.

Baseboard

Baseboard 'Carcass':

This model's baseboard is flat with no slopes or gradient. It is a low, inverted, 5 sided MDF or plywood box, clad with polystyrene sheet.

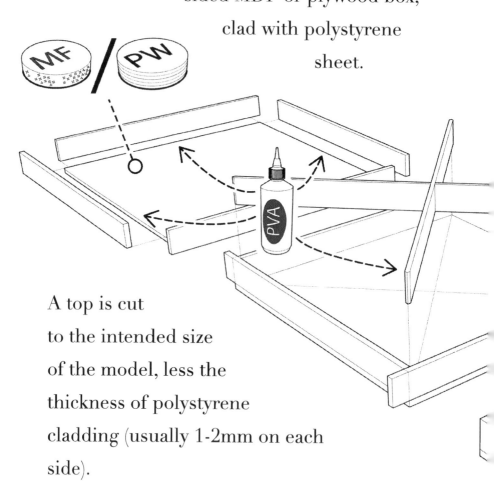

A top is cut to the intended size of the model, less the thickness of polystyrene cladding (usually 1-2mm on each side).

Sides are cut as strips that are slightly over length.

'Cross-bracing' is cut from the same strips to be fixed to the underside of the base. These are fixed together with PVA glue and held together with clamps or masking tape while the glue sets.

The overhanging sides are cut back and sanded to a smooth flat finish.

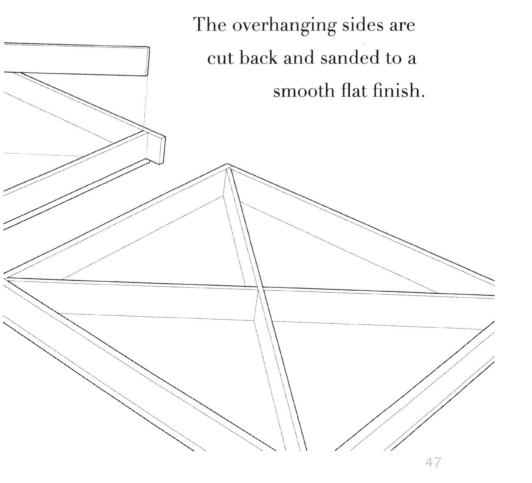

'Cladding':

Panels of polystyrene sheet are cut to fit onto the top and sides of the baseboard carcass.

As with the timber of the 'carcass', these panels are cut and fixed 'over length' and trimmed and sanded to a smooth finish once adhesive has set.

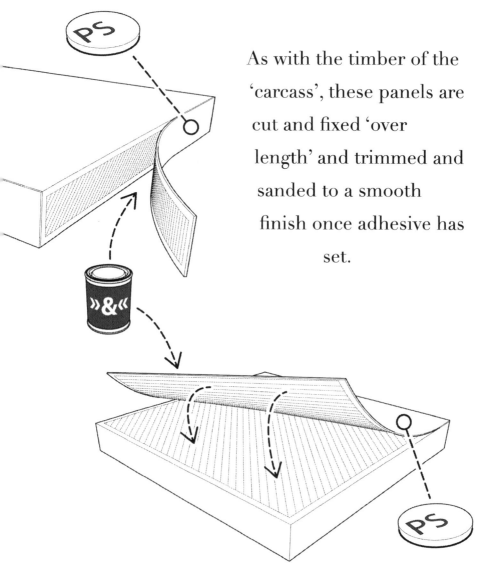

Tip: A handheld electric router with a trimming bit can be used to quickly trim the top and sides of larger baseboards. Contact adhesive should be applied so that a strip is left clear around the edge. This will avoid risk of the glue clogging sanding blocks or cutting bits.

The strips are glued with solvent, for plastic to plastic joints, and 'superglue' or contact adhesive, for plastic to timber joints. This will avoid glue being visible on the outside of the joints once sanded smooth.

Tip: Fixing the top first, and trimming to size, before adding the sides, will reduce the number of joints that will be visible as some will be covered with pavement pads later.

Pavements and surface detail:

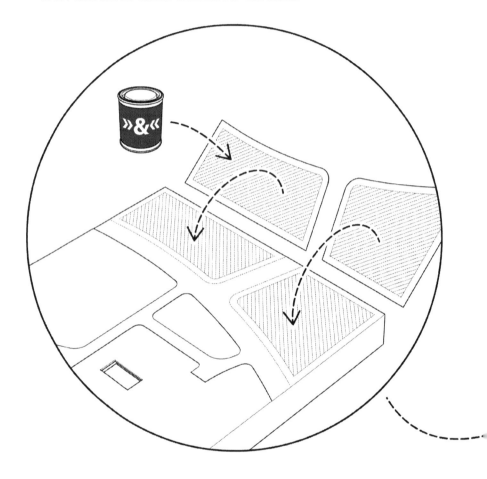

Detail is added to the top with polystyrene sheet 'pavements'. Detail to represent the patterns of paving, patios etc. is engraved into the surface of the polystyrene 'pavement' with a laser cutter.

All edges of the pavements are fixed with solvent. This is important to ensure that there is no risk of plastic panels distorting and buckling over time or due to the effects of any solvent in paint used for finishing.

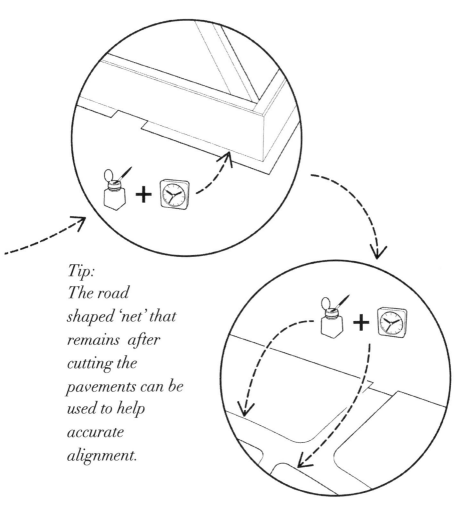

Tip:
The road shaped 'net' that remains after cutting the pavements can be used to help accurate alignment.

Water:

A swimming pool is represented by 'sinking' a block of clear acrylic into the structure of the baseboard, giving the appearance of water depth. This aperture is cut accurately into the polystyrene sheet of the baseboard top, with a larger hole cut into the MDF below to allow for accurate positioning.

The edges and base of this clear acrylic block are painted to represent the walls of the pool. The top is left clear to show the 'depth' of the pool.

Tip: Fixing the pool in place once the rest of the baseboard has been painted will avoid the need to mask the water's surface, and therefore allow a better finish.

Tip: This method works well for small areas of water. Larger areas can be better represented by adding a layer of 'back painted' clear acrylic to the top of the baseboard 'carcass' and shaping the polystyrene cladding to reveal it where needed.

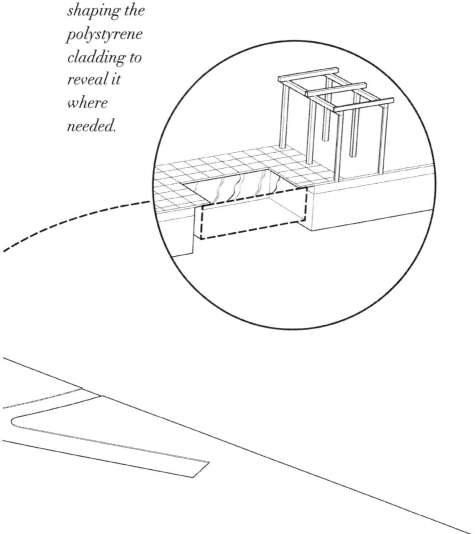

'Site'

Basics:

Since the purpose of this model is to introduce how a new building will fit into the existing context, it is appropriate that the 'site' is modeled in a relatively high level of detail. It is the only part of the area being modeled that is not available, in reality, to see.

This site consists of a barn conversion style building, matching 'garage block', an enclosed garden with a swimming pool and a pergola.

Sometimes context buildings will be made to this level of detail, especially at larger scales. The most detailed context buildings differ only in not having clear windows. This detail is what makes the 'site' more time consuming to build.

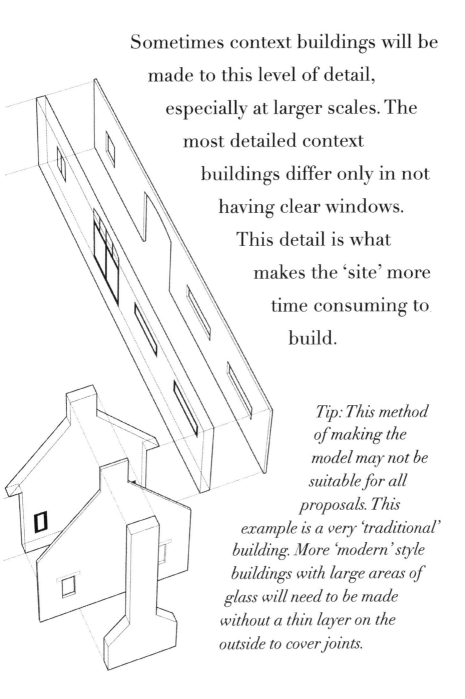

Tip: This method of making the model may not be suitable for all proposals. This example is a very 'traditional' building. More 'modern' style buildings with large areas of glass will need to be made without a thin layer on the outside to cover joints.

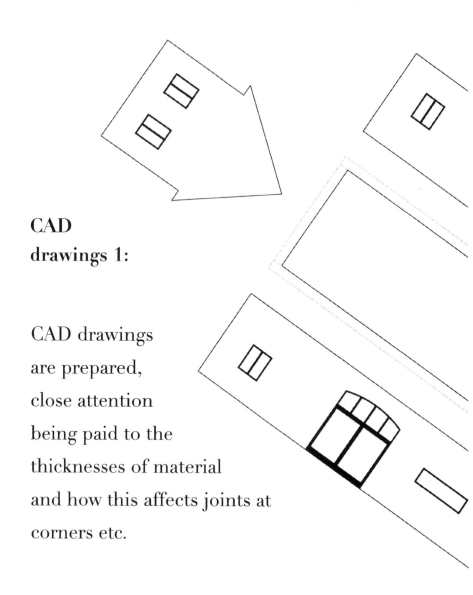

CAD drawings 1:

CAD drawings are prepared, close attention being paid to the thicknesses of material and how this affects joints at corners etc.

Tip: Labels can be etched into the 2 mm pieces to identify them easily. These labels will be covered later by other detail. This can be very useful if a model has many different buildings.

2 mm acrylic sheet is used for the main 'box' of the building and 0.5 mm acrylic for elevation detail. Both of these are laser cut using CAD data to ensure that apertures in the 0.5 mm elevations register correctly with etched window detail on

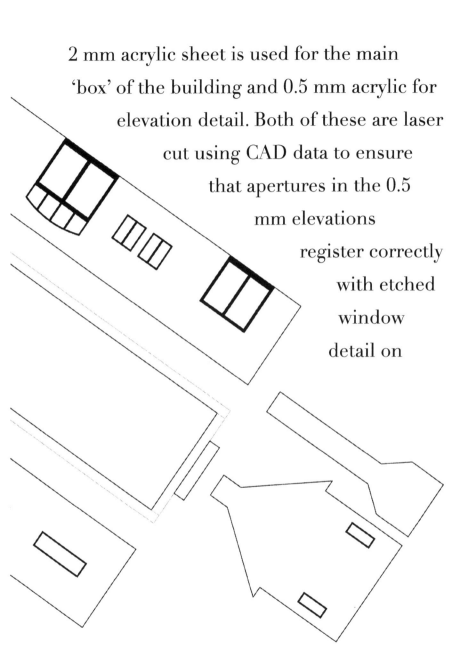

the main 2mm clear acrylic 'box' beneath.

Notches in the gable ends of the 'box' enable corner joints to register easily and squarely with the top of the side elevations. Details such as chimneys and roof lights are drawn at this stage, and cut with the larger pieces, to aid planning and cut down the number of times that the laser cutter must be set up.

Window detail is drawn so as to be etched into the 2 mm acrylic sheet with the laser cutter's 'rastering' technique.

Tip: 'Polylines' can be used in place of fill or hatch textures for ease of drawing and reliability when moving between different software packages.

Different thicknesses of line are used to achieve the necessary result. At smaller scales this level of detail, etched frames and a window cut in the elevation is plenty to explain what the elevation will look like.

Tip: At larger scales, when the elevation will be cut from thicker material, an additional layer might be used to fully represent the widows layout. For instance, if the elevation is cut from 1.5 mm sheet, it may be appropriate to add 0.5 mm thick detail inside the window aperture.

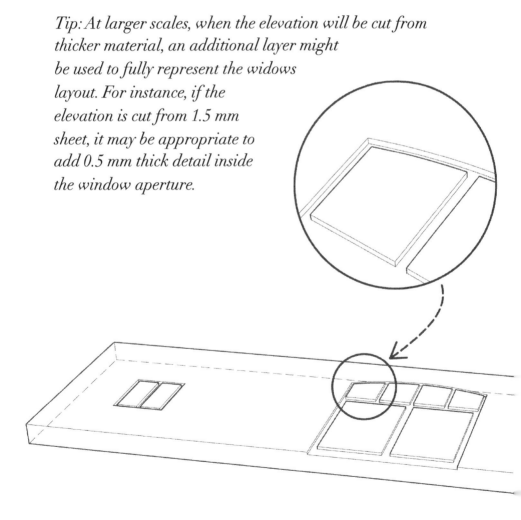

CAD drawings 2:

0.5 mm acrylic is etched and cut to form the elevations. Window apertures are cut out and details such as lintels, window sills and timber cladding are etched.

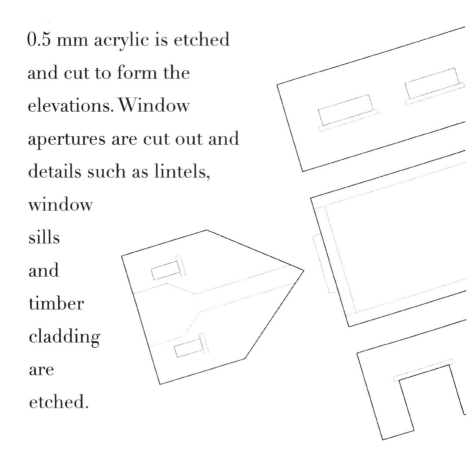

Elevations are made longer by about 1-2 mm at either end to allow for sanding back to neat corners.

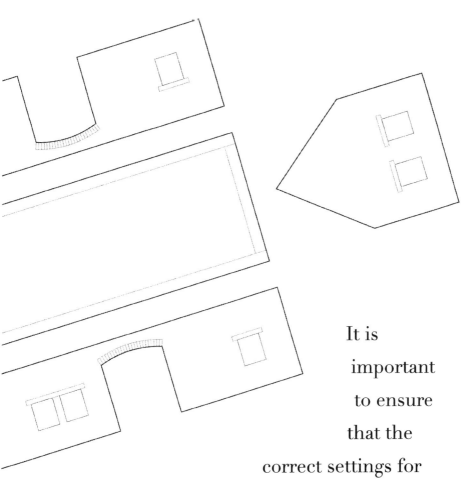

It is important to ensure that the correct settings for the material being cut are used when setting up the laser cutter. This will ensure that cuts are accurate and consistent. Different materials require different settings to ensue a good quality finish when laser cut.

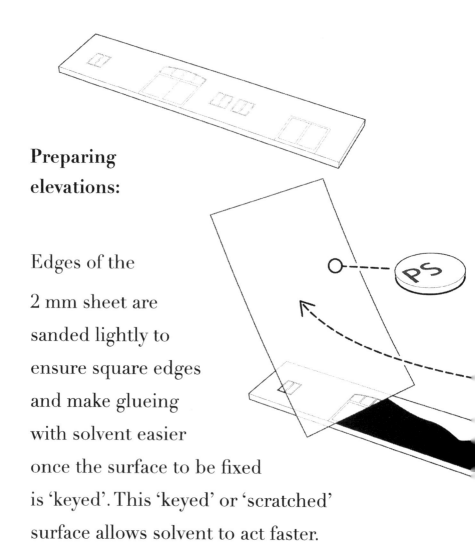

Preparing elevations:

Edges of the 2 mm sheet are sanded lightly to ensure square edges and make glueing with solvent easier once the surface to be fixed is 'keyed'. This 'keyed' or 'scratched' surface allows solvent to act faster.

Acrylic paint is rubbed into the etched window detail with a brush or a small polystyrene 'spatula'. As polystyrene is softer than acrylic there is little risk of scratching.

Acrylic paint is affected less by solvent than cellulose or enamel during assembly. Acrylic paint is also softer, enabling excess to be removed more easily.

Excess paint is removed with a polystyrene scraper to leave paint in the window detail and the 'glass' clear.

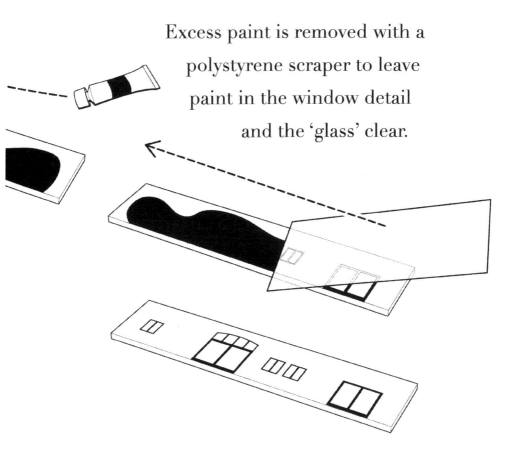

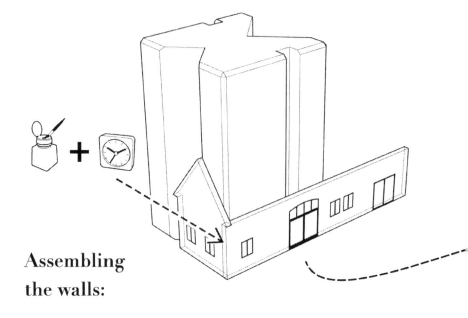

Assembling the walls:

The main walls of the building are assembled. Engineer's squares and blocks are used to ensure that the 'box' remains square.

It is important at this stage to assemble the walls on a smooth flat surface so that they remain in correct alignment. Pieces are placed together 'dry' and solvent offered to the joint with a brush.

It is important that each joint is fixed accurately so that elevations can be added easily later.

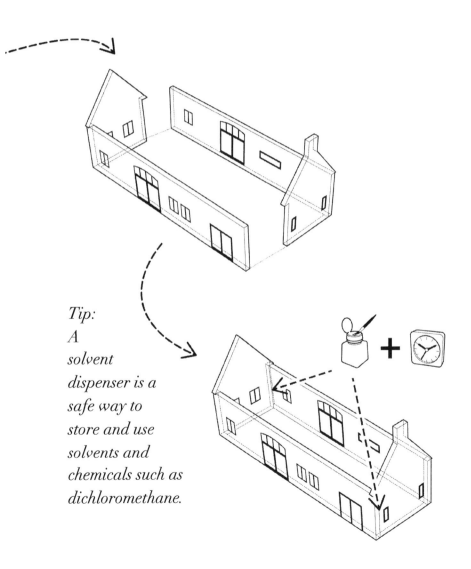

*Tip:
A solvent dispenser is a safe way to store and use solvents and chemicals such as dichloromethane.*

Elevations:

Elevations are added, ensuring careful alignment of the window detail. The extra 1-2 mm, added to one or both ends of each elevation is sanded back to make a neat corner. A little filler may be needed to blend elevations around the corners.

It is important that no line is visible here as it will 'give away' the construction of the model and suggest detail in the building that is not there in reality.

Chimney detail is added to an end elevation by fixing further thicknesses of acrylic cut the right shape. Care is taken to ensure that it lines up correctly with the shape of the end of the building.

Tip: Registration marks can be etched into the elevations to aid location of details like chimneys. This can be especially helpful if a detail does not sit against an edge that it can be lined up with.

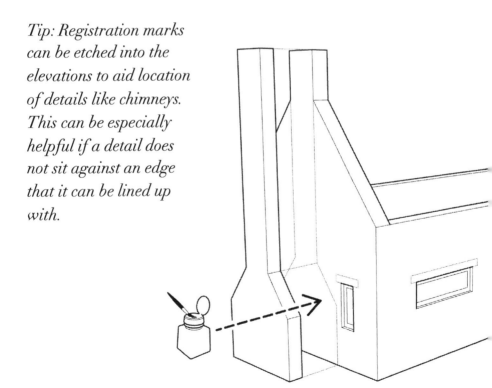

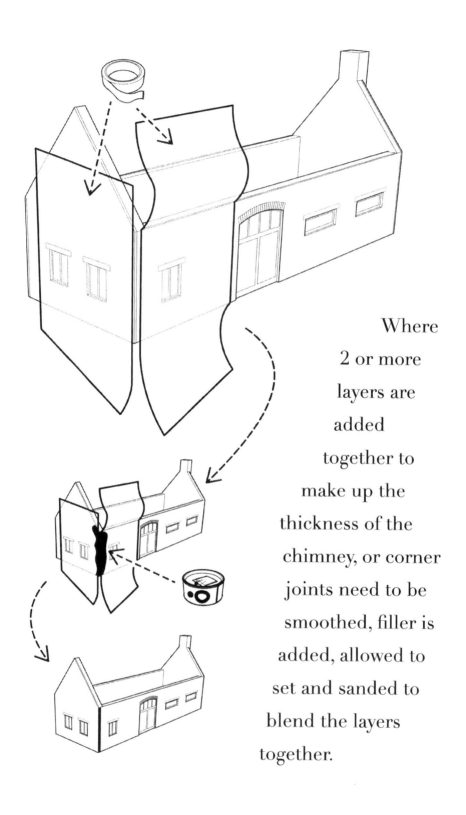

Where 2 or more layers are added together to make up the thickness of the chimney, or corner joints need to be smoothed, filler is added, allowed to set and sanded to blend the layers together.

Strips of masking tape are laid, onto the elevations, either side of the area to be filled. Once filler is applied, and before it sets, the tape can be removed, taking with it any excess filler. This will leave less to sand, reducing the possibility of rounding corners, or damaging the etched in detail above the windows, with the sanding block.

Care is taken to ensure that none of the etched detail on the outer elevations is obscured by filler.

Tip: Filler should always applied with the aim of leaving as little as possible to be sanded off again. Some fine surface fillers, especially those that are water based, need very little sanding to smooth them.

Roof:

Roof panels are cut from textured polystyrene sheet. The tile pattern of the sheet can be used to help marking out for cutting the apertures for roof lights.

Tip: To reduce the chance of mistakes due to measuring, mark the roof panels for cutting around the chimney by laying them in place and marking carefully with a scalpel, rather than measuring and transferring dimensions to the material.

Since polystyrene sheet cannot be reliably cut with a laser, the roof-lights are cut out by hand, with a drill and sharp scalpel.

The edges of the apertures are marked out with light scalpel marks. Holes are drilled at the corner of each window and 'linked together' by cutting with a sharp scalpel.

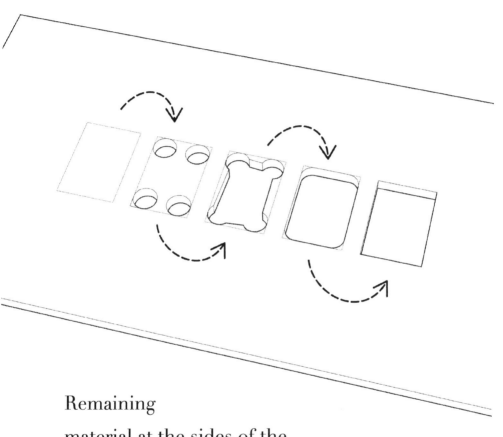

Remaining material at the sides of the apertures and the corners is removed by careful 'paring', again with a sharp scalpel.

Roof windows:

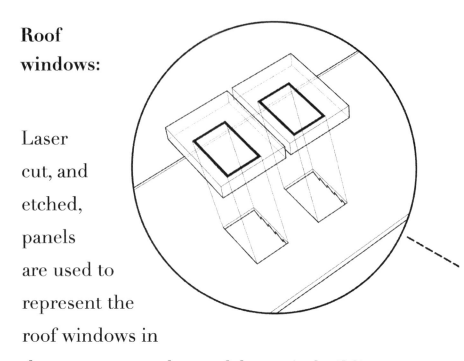

Laser cut, and etched, panels are used to represent the roof windows in the same way as those of the main building. Paint is rubbed in, and the windows are fixed to the underside of the polystyrene roof panels in the correct places.

These will not be visible through the ground floor windows of the building since it will be fixed to baseboard.

Tip: A simple white polystyrene wall can be added to obscure the view through building. No extra detail is usually needed at small scales. The lack of a clear view through the model is enough to give the impression that there is detail inside.

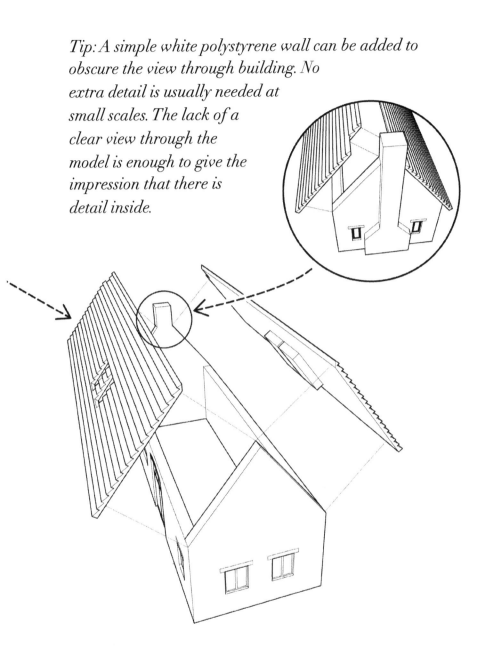

Ridge Tiles:

Ridge detail is added as one piece of angle section polystyrene strip, fixed with solvent.

Tip: To avoid the need to measure accurately, cut the angle strip over length and trim it to fit once the solvent has set.

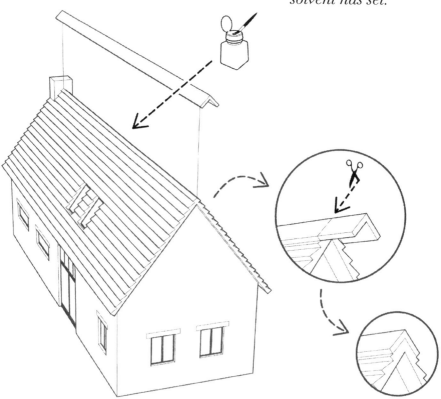

Masking:

In preparation for painting the model, windows are masked with tape. Tape is laid into the window apertures and pushed gently into the edges with a suitable tool. The tape can be cut very accurately by running a sharp scalpel along the edge of the window aperture.

Tip: Masking tape could be cut with the laser cutter to the right shape for each window (the same CAD data that created the elevations can be used).

Tape is applied carefully to ensure that none is lifting up, especially at the corner of windows, as this will result in overspray of paint onto the clear windows.

Painting:

The model is temporarily fixed, with double sided tape, to a scrap of timber board for painting. This means that the model can be moved around for painting without touching the model itself.

Care is taken to hold the model so that all parts of it can be painted as easily as possible. If more than one colour is to be applied, the order that the colours are sprayed should be worked out so that lighter colours and / or areas that are easiest to mask are sprayed first.

A thin coat of primer is applied. A fine surface filler is used to make good any remaining blemishes.

Tip: A water based 'fine surface filler' can be sanded very easily. This is advantageous at this stage as there is a danger of damaging small details if vigorous sanding is needed.

Tip: It is a good idea to arrange construction of the model so that most pieces can be painted at the same time. This will reduce the number of times that the spray gun will need to be cleaned and help the final coat of pain to be a consistent colour across the model.

Masking tape is carefully removed. The model is checked for problems, then set aside to be added to the baseboard later.

Summary:

The garage block next to the main site serves as a summary.

A laser cutter is used

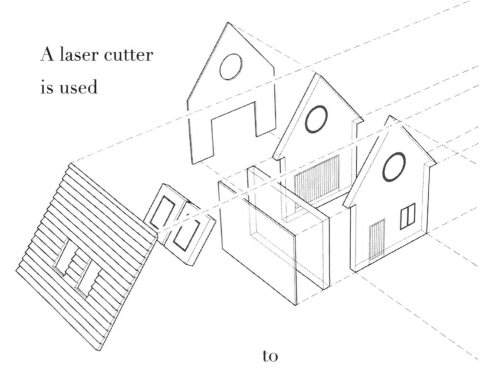

to create 2mm acrylic panels that are etched with window detail. The window frame detail is filled with paint to represent window and door detail. These panels are assembled into a box that is then wrapped with 0.5mm acrylic that has window apertures cut from it and further detail etched into it.

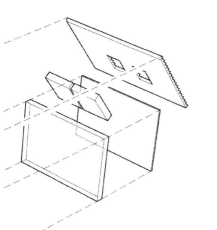

This box is carefully finished to hide any visible joins at the corners.

The roof is represented with panels of pre-textured styrene. Apertures cut into these enable further 2mm acrylic panels to represent roof windows.

Context 1

It is important to consider the intended use of the model, and its audience, when deciding what the appropriate level of detail for it is. The example used in this book is assumed to be a model made to demonstrate the appearance of a new development and enable the viewer to understand how this will relate to an existing context.

The audience for this model are not all architects / designers or those familiar with more abstract models. Therefore the model is made in a style that is simplified enough to be economical and also realistic enough to be 'read' by its audience.

The context for the 'site' is represented by modeling the 'massing' of surrounding buildings. Some are modeled with a high level of detail to capture their character and make them easily recognisable, others are more simply represented as they are less important or further away from the 'site'.

Walls and trees help to make the scale of the model clear and enable those viewing the model to easily relate the model to reality.

This book does not consider the colour of the finished model. This may be a very important factor for some models, but this example is intended to illustrate the design and construction of the model. This model will follow the established convention of the 'all white architect's model'. This convention being used to emphasise form, massing and, sometimes, texture, rather than the realistic appearance of the finished building.

Good practice when making context blocks:

- Context buildings should be created by adding smaller blocks together, not by removing material from a larger block.
- Sand small blocks to a smooth finish before joining them to make more complicated 'sub-assemblies'.
- Avoid sanding inside corners to a smooth finish. Arrange pieces so that all blocks have outside corners and edges, and are brought together after sanding smooth (and sometimes painting).
- Where many similar pieces are needed, long extrusions should be cut of the necessary shape and cut into shorter lengths. This will reduce the number of cut to be made.

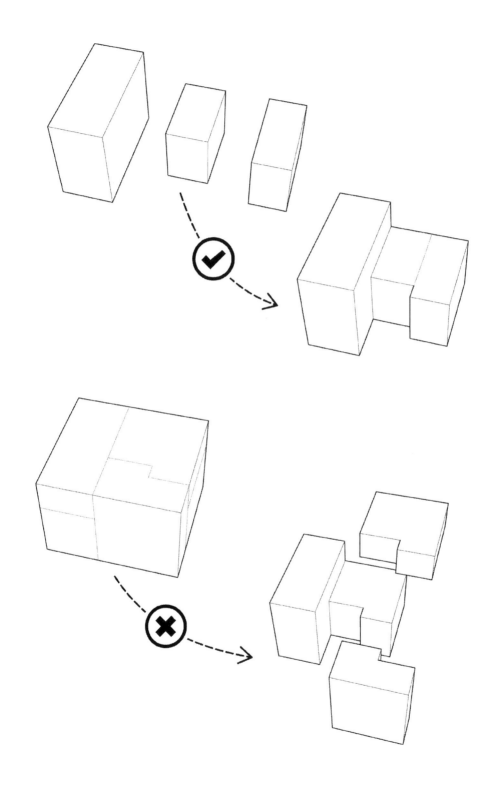

- When multiples of the same 'block' are needed, a jig should be set to enable them to be made at the same time. Aim to only set tools once.

- Styrene strips are available that can be used to represent many details, saving the time taken to cut material down to size. Cornices, door surrounds, steps etc. can all be made using these ready made strips.

- Larger buildings may be best made as hollow boxes (like the 'site') to save material and weight. These boxes can be detailed with smaller blocks and styrene strips etc.

- At very small scales, groups of buildings can be represented by simple, plates. Models of urban areas might show whole city blocks as one piece.

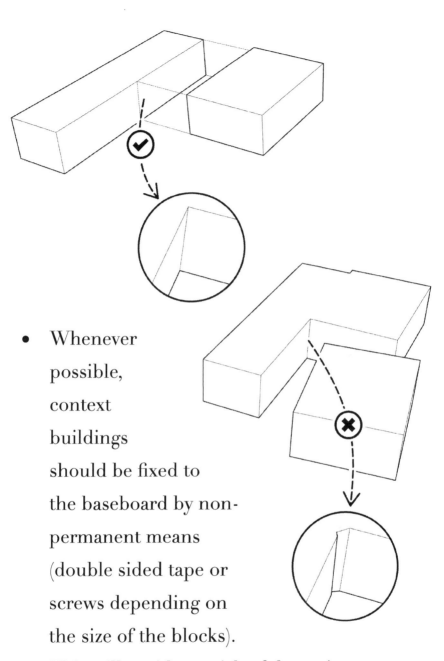

- Whenever possible, context buildings should be fixed to the baseboard by non-permanent means (double sided tape or screws depending on the size of the blocks). This will avoid any risk of damaging finishes with glue or if changes need to made.

Simplest context buildings:

Small barns and garages are modeled on one edge of the baseboard. These are blocks of model board cut to represent the basic massing of the buildings.

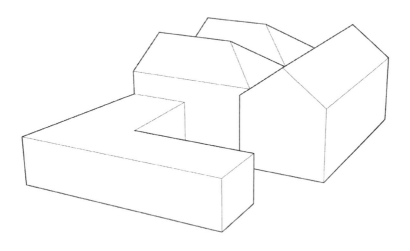

These are modeled with an accurate ground plan, simplified roof shapes and no detail to the elevations.

Basic roof profiles:

Blocks are cut to the correct shape for the plan of the buildings.

The pitch of the roofs are cut with a table saw set the the relevant angle. With the base of the building against the fence of the saw, a series of cuts are made with each elevation against the bed in turn.

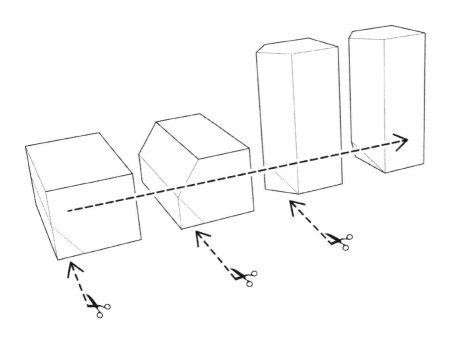

Planning Ahead:

Care is taken to plan the construction of context blocks so that they can be made efficiently and as 'crisply' as possible. Time taken to plan and construct blocks like these in a suitable way will avoid more difficult remedial work later.

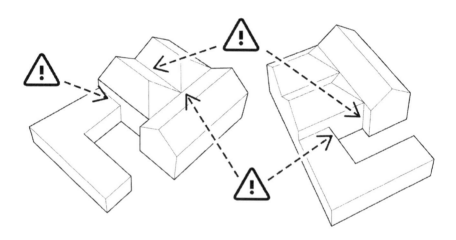

In this example there are several inside corners that can be avoided and buildings that have the same pitched roofs can be represented with sections cut from one long extrusion.

Model board blocks are glued together with 'super glue', being sure to avoid creating inside corners until the blocks have been sanded cleanly. Some blocks, though, are sanded after gluing together to enable joins to be made smooth.

At this stage the buildings are made oversize at one side, to overhang the edge of the baseboard.

Assembly:

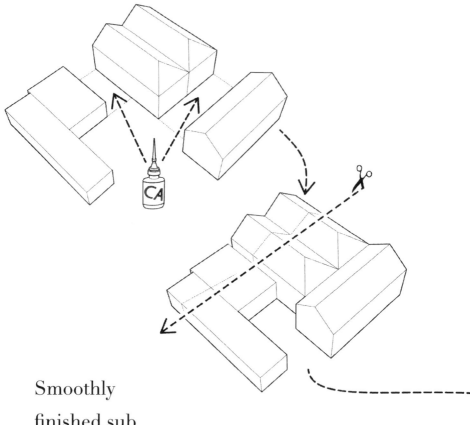

Smoothly finished sub assemblies are glued together with 'super-glue'.

Tip: It may be advantageous not to join some buildings together, even if they fit together on the finished model, if they are easier to spray paint individually. It is difficult to spray into inside corners and 'holes' that are surrounded by blocks.

Finally, the building is cut to fit the baseboard. Held in the correct position, the building is marked with a scalpel cut or sharp pencil.

A bandsaw is used to cut roughly to size, an accurate fit being achieved with a circular sander. A fine sanding block is used for final finishing, ready for painting.

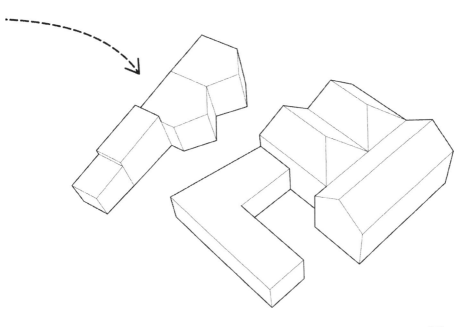

Simple Barn Buildings:

A barn is represented as simple blocks, but with more detailed roofs, as it lies next to the site.

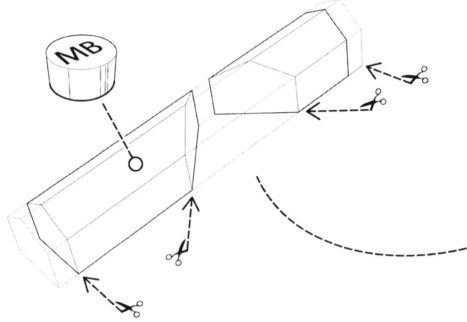

A block of model board is cut to the profile of these buildings. This block is slightly longer than needed to allow for cutting to exact size with some room for error. A 'mitre' joint is arranged at the centre of the block. The model board blocks are fixed together with 'super-glue'.

Roof detail is represented with polystyrene sheet. These panels are arranged to overhang the sides of the block slightly, to represent the eaves of the roof.

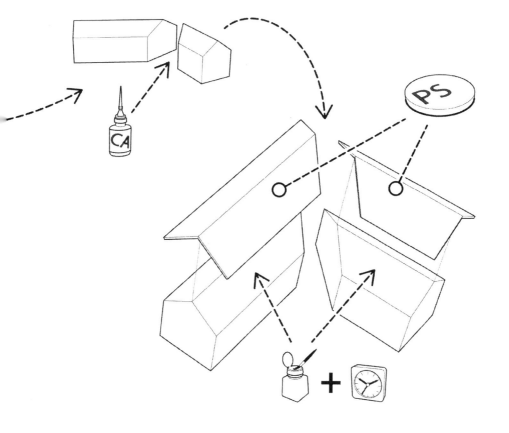

Bungalow:

A small bungalow is represented with more detail than the simplest blocks.

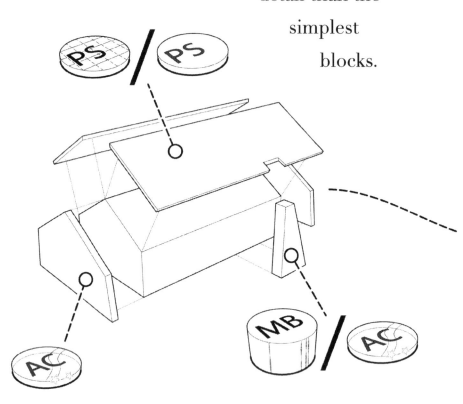

A block of model board is cut to the roof profile, acrylic panels are added to each end to represent the 'buttress detail'. A chimney is represented with either a block cut from thicker acrylic or a small block of model board.

Roof detail is represented with polystyrene sheet. A notch is needed to enable this to fit around the chimney. This is marked out and cut with a sharp scalpel.

Tip: Marking the material with a sharp scalpel will avoid any pencil or ink marks remaining on the model that might show through paint. Marking direct from the model, rather than measuring from a drawing, reduces the risk of mistakes.

Ridge tiles are not represented, as the level of detail is kept low. A simple mitre is sanded, in the styrene panels, where they meet at the ridge of the roof.

Cutting model-board blocks:

A small barn is modeled as a simple block, but with the addition of some surface detail to represent more of its character. The door is represented by a recess in the side elevation, the prominent 'step' around the base is added and steps to a door at high level on one side are shown.

A block of model board is shaped to form the basic shape of the barn. 1 mm polystyrene 'elevations' will be added in this instance, so the model board block is made 1 mm smaller on each side that will receive one.

Tip: It is often easier to add an elevation to all sides of the block, even if there are no apertures to be shown, to simplify the measurements of the block, and provide a consistent surface for painting.

Blocks are best cut with a table saw. After cutting with the saw, sanding blocks are used to smooth the faces of the model board.

It is very important to be sure that the surface of the model board is ready to take a paint finish before any further detail is added. It is much easier to finish the whole of each face when it is flat and smooth.

Sanding, for instance, the inside of window apertures after the elevations are fixed down is much more difficult and greatly increases the risk of damaging other fine detail.

Roof shape:

The roof shape is created by cutting the block with a table saw set to the correct angle.

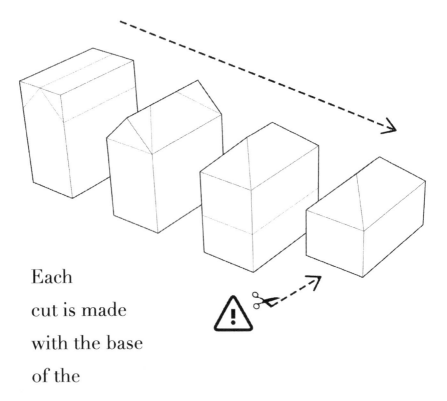

Each cut is made with the base of the building against the fence and each of the elevations facing down in turn. Again, sanding blocks are used to smooth the newly cut surfaces.

Later, textured polystyrene sheet will be used to finish the roof so there is no need for a perfect finish, the aim should be to provide a flat surface for adhesive to 'grip' later.

Tip: To cut roofs steeper than 45° the block cannot be cut with its base against the fence and a flat side running on the bed of the saw. To achieve steeper pitches the block is fixed to another, larger, block with double sided tape and cut upside down. Because only one cut can be made before the block is removed, turned and re-fixed, pitches close to 45° will often be simplified to 45° to save time.

Elevation detail:

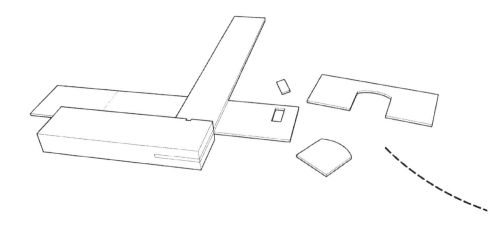

Elevations can be cut by hand (in polystyrene sheet) or with a laser cutter (in acrylic sheet). For complicated buildings it may be preferable to first draw the elevations with CAD software for accuracy and the chance to rectify mistakes without remaking parts.

An extra 1-2 mm is added to one or both ends of each elevation to allow for sanding back to a neat corner. Elevations are fixed with suitable adhesive (contact adhesive for those with no, or few, apertures and solvent for others). Adhesive is allowed to fully cure before joints can be filled and carefully sanded smooth.

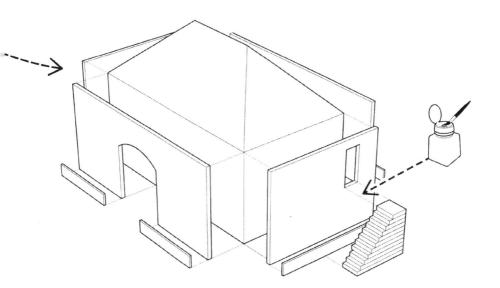

A sanding block is used to blend the top of the applied elevations into the roof pitch in preparation for adding roof detail.

Roof detail / texture:

Roof detail is added with pre-textured polystyrene sheet. These sheets are available in textures that can be used to represent brick, tile, boarding, slates etc.

The shape of the panels is marked out either by measuring from the model or by drawing around the roof plane to be covered while holding it in place against the model board block. Each panel is cut, and checked for good fit, before fixing with suitable adhesive.

Ridge tile strips may be added as before. Five strips can be used to make up the right detail. Gaps where strips of ridge tile do not meet perfectly are filled with one part cellulose filler, smoothed with solvent and a suitable (non-precious) brush.

Tip: At smaller scales miter joints can be arranged to avoid the need for, possibly over-scale, ridge tile detail. these joints can be smoothed with one-part cellulose filler. At smaller scales it is more common for roofs to be represented with smooth sheet, making joints easier to fill and smooth.

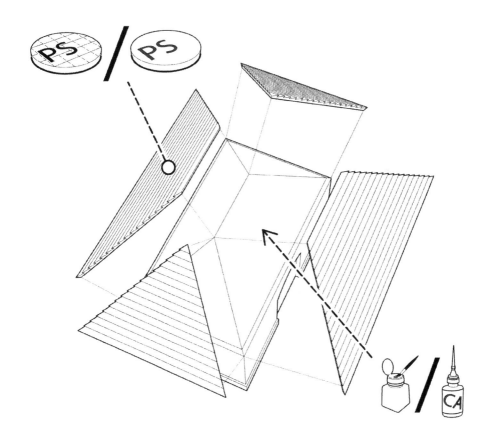

Steps:

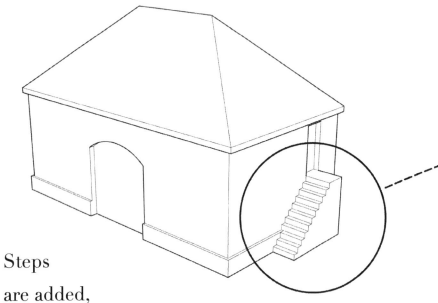

Steps are added, made with polystyrene strip overlapped and glued with solvent. The rough side is filled with one part cellulose filler and sanded smooth. Plinth detail is added with polystyrene strip fixed around the base of the building with solvent.

It is important to leave solvent and filler to fully cure before sanding smooth.

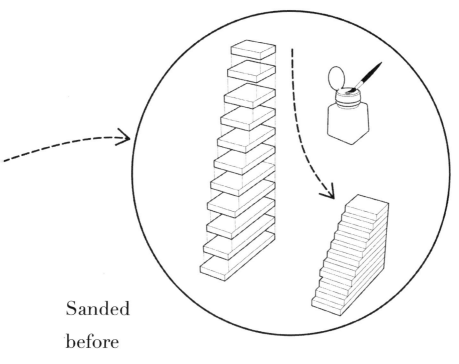

Sanded before fully cured, the filler will be 'dragged' out or clog sanding blocks. Sanding blocks clogged with soft filler cannot easily be cleaned, needing to be resurfaced with fresh sanding paper.

Chapel:

A large chapel sits opposite the site in one corner of the baseboard. It is also represented as a solid block with added elevation detail, but more layers are used to make up the elevations and to represent 'deeper' detail.

Today it may be common to make some of the detail shown in the chapel model with a CNC router / mill. It is often just as fast and effective to use this more traditional method, as no time is needed to set up the machine.

This choice of techniques will usually be made depending on the equipment available to the modelmaker.

Cutting blocks for the chapel:

Model board is cut to the shape of the main pitched roof. A slice is cut from one end and trimmed either side to make a block that is the same height but the correct width for the 'entrance' detail at the front of the building.

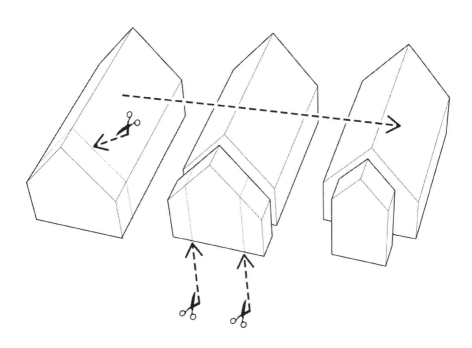

Chapel elevations:

Elevations for the chapel are cut from 'High Tolerance' Acrylic sheet with a laser cutter. Detail at the front of the chapel is created by building up layers of different shaped elevations that together make up the stepped detail around the door, and the window above.

Tip: It is a good idea to set up the CAD data for laser cutting the elevations so that the order that lines are cut can be controlled. This can help keep window aperture in correct alignment, avoid the build up of heat in one area of a sheet of plastic and enable more efficient nesting of parts.

Tip: More complex forms can be modeled by combining elevations of different thicknesses, pieces of polystyrene strip and blocks of acrylic / model-board.

The window apertures are cut out of the acrylic sheet first, followed by the outlines of the elevations. This ensures that there is no chance of the pieces moving, in the machine, as the outlines cut, leaving the window aperture out of alignment.

The outside edges of the elevations are used to align each layer onto the one behind.

Chapel assembly:

The chapel building is assembled by fixing 'layers' together in turn.

Tip: Model-board blocks should be sanded smooth, ready to be painted, before fixing elevations. If not it will not be possible to sand cleanly inside the window apertures.

Acrylic elevations are fixed to model board with small amounts of 'super-glue' at the centre of the elevations and solvent around the edges. Acrylic pieces are fixed to each other with solvent.

Tip: While it is usually good practice to cut elevation detail slightly over length, to allow for sanding to size later, the kind of detail included in the chapel can be more easily aligned if cut to the right size initially. Fine filler or one part cellulose filler can be used to smooth any visible joins.

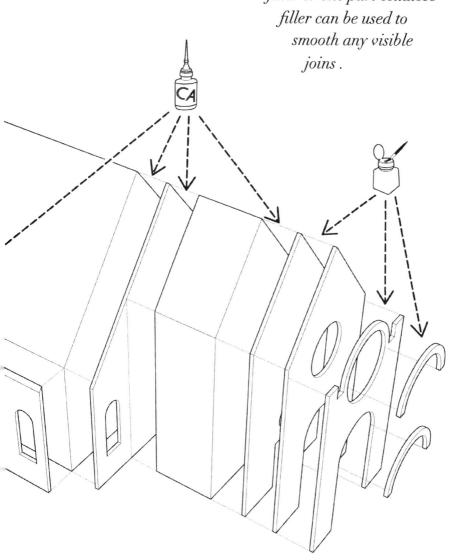

Chapel roof panels:

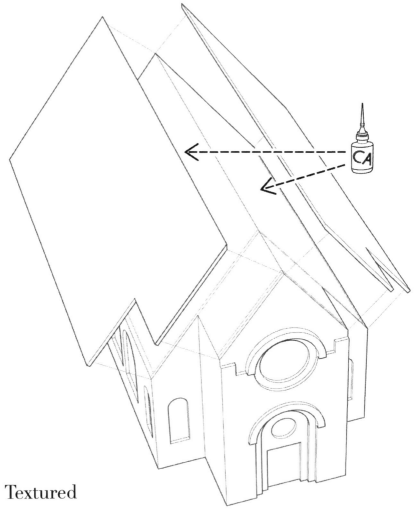

Textured polystyrene sheet is cut to fit the shape of the building and fixed with 'super-glue' in the centre of the panels and solvent around the edge to avoid distortion.

Tip: Many sheet materials will bend if painted on just one side. This is more likely to happen to materials, like polystyrene, that are vulnerable to the solvents in paint. This risk can be minimised by fixing down the whole surface of panels or painting both sides.

A polystyrene strip may added to the top of the roof to represent ridge tiles and hide any visible join between the two panels.

In this case the strip is omitted, so that the level of detail in the chapel is lower than that of other buildings that are closer to the 'site'.

Cutting to fit the baseboard:

The chapel needs to be cut to fit properly against the edge of the baseboard.

The model is held in place on the baseboard ensuring that it is in the correct location. At the edge of the baseboard a mark is made at the bottom edge of each side that overhangs the baseboard and the model is cut and sanded carefully to the correct shape.

It is important that the 'cut line' through the building at the edge of the baseboard is flat and perpendicular to the baseboard surface. To make this possible a circular sander must be well set up to ensure that it is accurate and square.

Context 3

Detailed context:

The most detailed context buildings on a model will usually be those that are important to the character of the area being modeled and those that are closest to the site.

These parts of the context will often be as detailed as the 'site' in order for them to have the same 'value'. In some cases the only difference in detail may be the inclusion of clear windows in the 'site'.

Sometimes it is important to show detail so that the viewer can understand the model by recognising familiar landmarks and the correct scale of the model.

Close to the 'site' is a large house with period detail that must be represented accurately to capture its character.

Chimneys, a complex front door, a small extension and decorative cornices have to be represented to fully capture the character of this building.

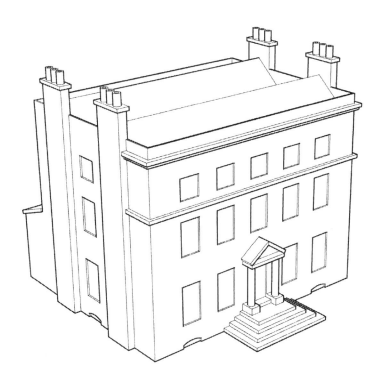

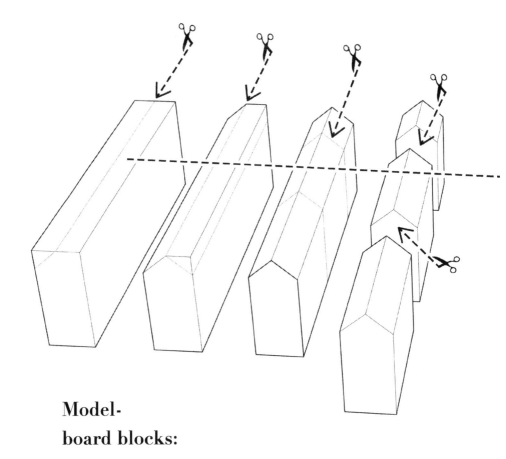

Model-board blocks:

Model board is cut to represent the main roof shape of the building. A long strip is cut with a pitched roof shape. This strip is deliberately cut a little longer than needed to allow room for error. This is cut into lengths that will come together to represent

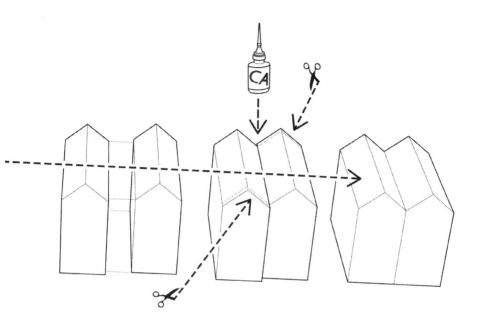

the 'double pitch'. Again these pieces are cut longer than needed to avoid the need to glue them together perfectly first time, since 'super glue' will cure instantly.

Finally the finished block is sanded to correct final dimensions, taking into account the thickness of elevations that will be added to represent facade detail.

Facades and chimneys:

Elevation detail is laser cut from 'High Tolerance' acrylic sheet. It is important that the model board surface below is sanded to a smooth finish before these are attached.

Parapet detail around the top of the building is represented by elevations that extend above the eaves of the roof. If needed, these could be thickened with the addition of another layer of polystyrene or thin acrylic to the back of the elevation where it sits above the roof.

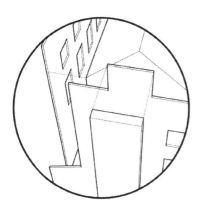 

'Extension':

Pieces of acrylic sheet (or model-board) form a block inside the 'extension'. Elevations are cut from 0.5mm acrylic sheet. Joins are filled, if necessary, and a roof panel of polystyrene or acrylic sheet is added.

Larger details like this could be assembled as a box clad with thin elevation detail, like the 'site'.

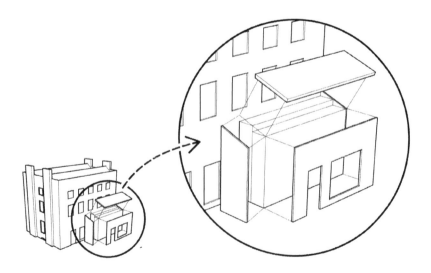

Tip: If thicknesses of acrylic sheet are not suitable for the size of a block like this, Thin polystyrene sheet 'packing' can be added behind.

Door detail:

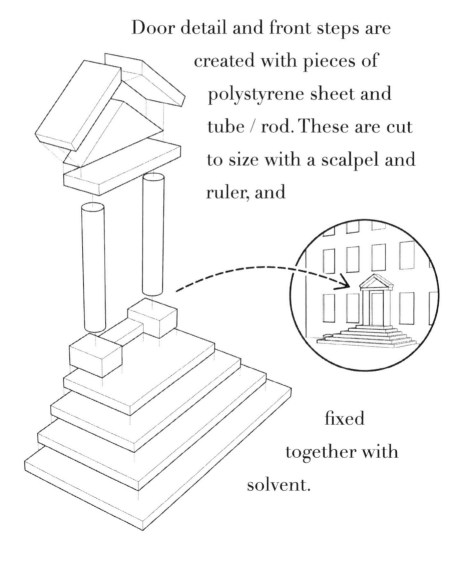

Door detail and front steps are created with pieces of polystyrene sheet and tube / rod. These are cut to size with a scalpel and ruler, and fixed together with solvent.

Tip: At larger scales it can be more effective to laser cut flat pieces from acrylic sheet for details like this as more detail could then be included.

Cornice detail:

Cornice detail is added to the elevations with polystyrene strip. This is held in place 'dry' and fixed by applying solvent with a brush, allowing it to be drawn into the joint by capillary action.

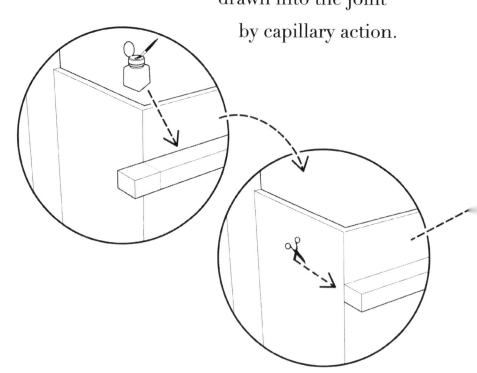

At each corner the strip is left slightly too long, the solvent left to set and then the strips are trimmed to size and sanded to an exact fit as needed.

Once the final strips are added the detail is very carefully sanded to make it appear as if made from one piece of plastic. The cornice is completed with strips of round section polystyrene strip added below the first rectangular section.

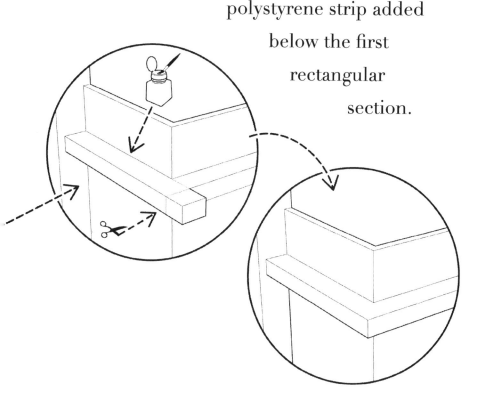

This method of combining different sections and sizes of polystyrene strips can be used to build many complex details that would be difficult to create as an extrusion before adding to the elevation. Gaps are filled with one part cellulose filler, brushed smooth with solvent.

Chimneys are represented by short lengths of polystyrene

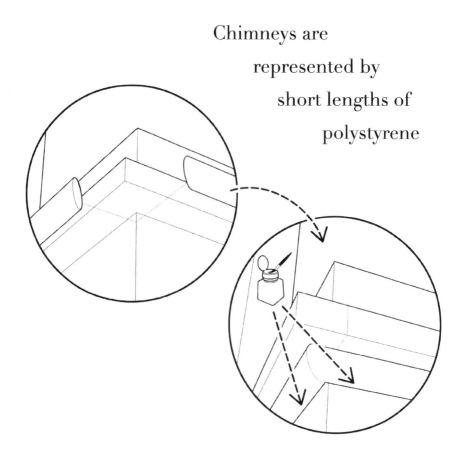

tube, fixed in place with solvent. These can be cut with a scalpel and sanded together, to make them all the same height, after fixing.

Tip: For white models use white tube to avoid the need to paint inside the chimneys. For coloured models dark grey tube can be used to represent the 'shadow' inside.

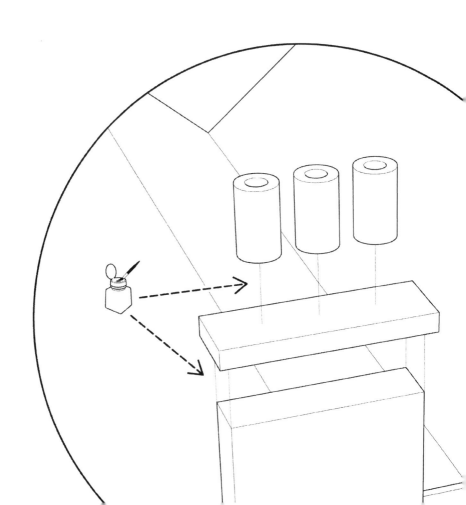

Open sided buildings:

An outbuilding in the grounds of the large period house has open sides and is modeled as below to represent its character accurately.

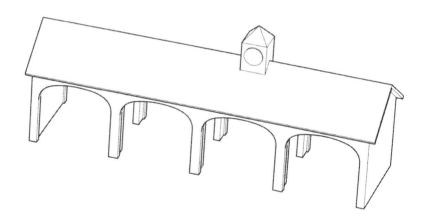

This building could be made as a block, with elevations added to show the detail, but is modeled 'open' to show how details can be made by combining techniques used, in this book, for 'context' and 'site'.

To ensure that the clock tower fits perfectly, filler is 'cast' to the shape of the roof. This method of casting polyester filler against tape, as a release agent is a very useful technique to make blocks fit together well.

Tip: A lot of time can be saved by cutting blocks roughly to shape, and slightly undersize, with a bandsaw and filling the resulting gap with 'cast' filler.

Tip: If tape can be made to conform to the shape closely enough, this method can be used to cast filler to fit against curved and irregular surfaces.

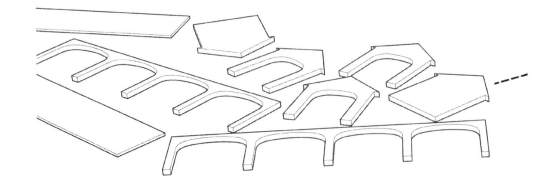

Assembly:

Elevations and 'cross sections' are drawn, with CAD software, and cut from acrylic sheet with a laser cutter.

Engineers blocks are used to hold the pieces together 'dry' and solvent applied to fix the joints. It is important that the model is held square as it is assembled to ensure that all the pieces fit together and the finished building is true. The roof is

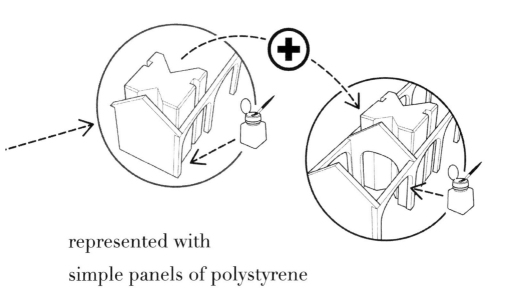

represented with simple panels of polystyrene sheet, fixed in place with solvent.

Tip: The shape of a building like this may be difficult to spray paint as air pressure will blow paint back out of the inside spaces. This can be helped by painting the model before adding the roof panels.

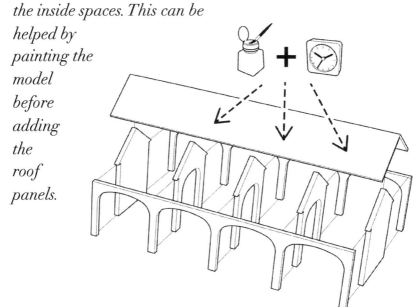

'Casting' detail to fit:

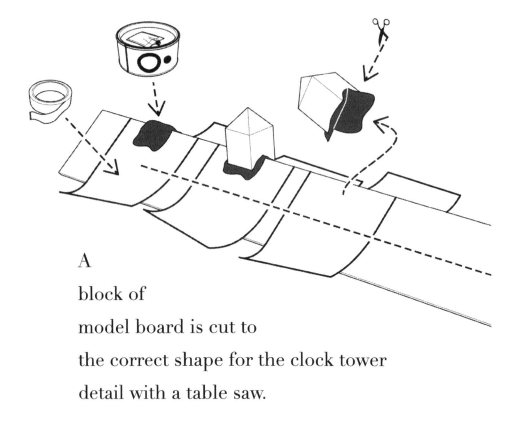

A block of model board is cut to the correct shape for the clock tower detail with a table saw.

The "point" of the roof is cut at one end of the block and the rough shape of the roof profile is cut into its base with a bandsaw. There is little need for this cut to be made very accurately, though it is always good practice to use as little filler as possible.

A short length of parcel tape is placed onto the roof of the building.

A small 'blob' of filler is prepared, placed onto the roof and the clock tower block pushed down into it. Once the filler has set, the tower can be removed, followed by the tape.

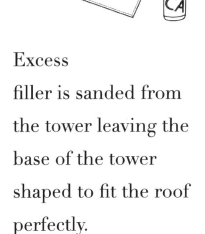

Excess filler is sanded from the tower leaving the base of the tower shaped to fit the roof perfectly.

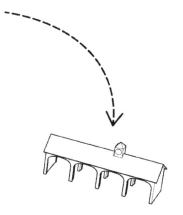

Tip: Since polyester filler will not stick well to plastic tapes, like parcel tape, it is a useful release agent for 'casting' details in polyester filler. Release agents recommended for mouldmaking should be avoided as the will often leave a greasy residue which will prevent paint adhering to the finished model.

A clock-face, of either polystyrene or acrylic sheet, is added and finally the tower is fixed to the roof with a small amount of 'super-glue'.

Trees:

Many models make use of ready made scale model trees that can be sourced from model shops and suppliers of modelmaking materials.

A large range of model trees are available to buy, 'ready to use'. These range from simple solid shapes, through 'bottle brush' or 'pipe cleaner' style trees to very realistic trees of etched brass and scale foliage.

When a large number of trees are needed, they can be very expensive if bought 'off the shelf'. This cost, however, will usually be less than the cost of a modelmaker's time that would be needed to make them.

Different qualities of realism and finish are available to suit different styles of presentation. For many models, accurate or realistic trees are not necessary, just a representation. This model will make use of simple twisted wire trees that can be made economically and easily, as few are needed.

Since trees for this model are considered 'representations', not accurate scale replicas. They follow the same kind of language that is applied to context buildings.

Tip: A great many things can be used to represent trees at different scales. At small scales it is easiest to model the whole canopy as one. At larger scales the level of detail should be judged carefully to be appropriate for the model.

Twisting wire:

Fine copper wire is stripped from electrical flex and cut into lengths of about twice the height of the finished tree. Groups of 3-4 of these lengths are twisted together, leaving short lengths untwisted at one end. This is repeated 8-9 times.

2-3 of these 'branches' are then twisted together, again leaving some of the length untwisted so that the branches gradually thin towards the top of the tree.

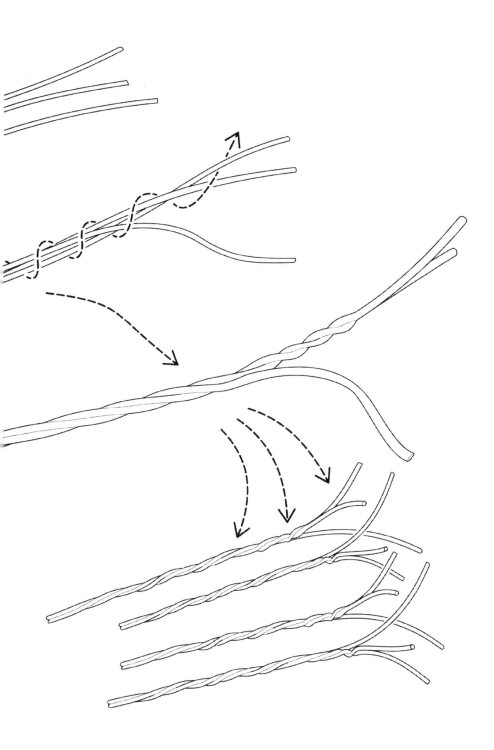

149

These groups of branches are twisted together, this time leaving a 'trunk' of twisted wire at the base of the tree.

A piece of thicker copper or brass wire, perhaps 1 - 1.5 mm thick, is carefully threaded into the centre of the trunk. This will be used to fix the tree to the base of the model by fixing it into a small hole.

Wire at the base of the tree is shaped into the trunk by wrapping excess around the trunk to thicken it at the base.

Finishing and 'planting':

Solder is used to strengthen the tree, since copper is well suited to this method. A soldering iron is used to heat up the copper wire until solder will flow into the twisted structure of the tree. Just enough solder is added to make sure that the tree is robust enough to withstand handling.

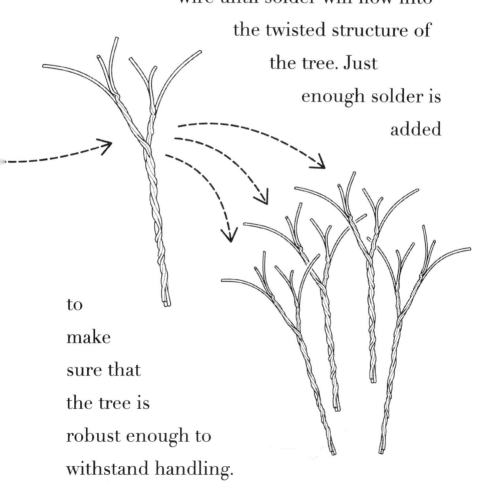

Tip: A little liquid flux painted onto the wire will help the solder to flow easily and reduce the chance of 'dry soldering'.

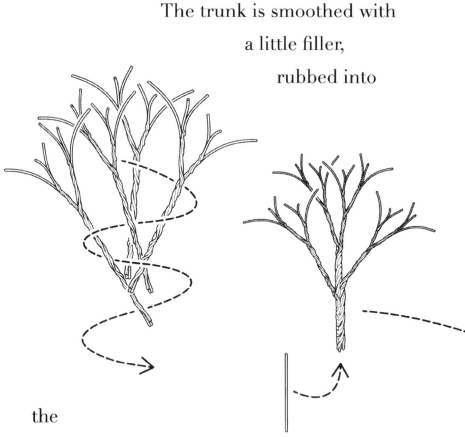

The trunk is smoothed with a little filler, rubbed into the twisted wire texture to disguise the method of construction. At the base of the tree enough filler is added to be able to cut a 'flat' base to the trunk.

Once the filler is set to a 'cheesy' consistency it is cut away with a scalpel to give a smooth flat base that will enable the tree to appear as if it is growing out of the baseboard once planted.

Branches are tweaked into the right shape,

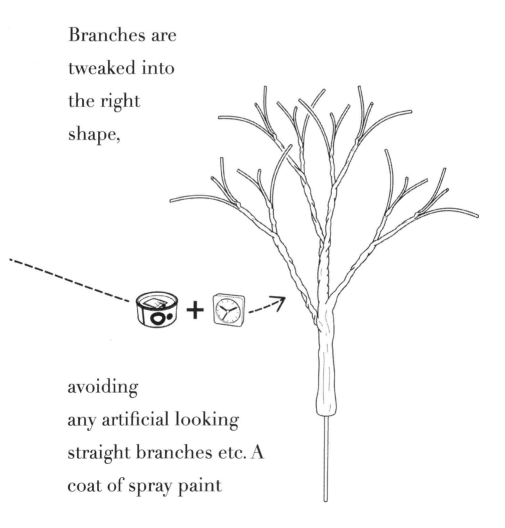

avoiding any artificial looking straight branches etc. A coat of spray paint finishes the tree in a suitable colour for the finished model.

Finally the tree is planted with the thicker wire 'stalk' glued into a hole that is just big enough in the base of the model.

P.V.A or emulsion glue should be used for fixing the trees.

Sometimes it can be preferable to simply bend over the 'stalk' of the tree, on the underside of the baseboard. The trees can then be removed, replaced or repositioned easily when changes are made to the finished model.

Walls and fences:

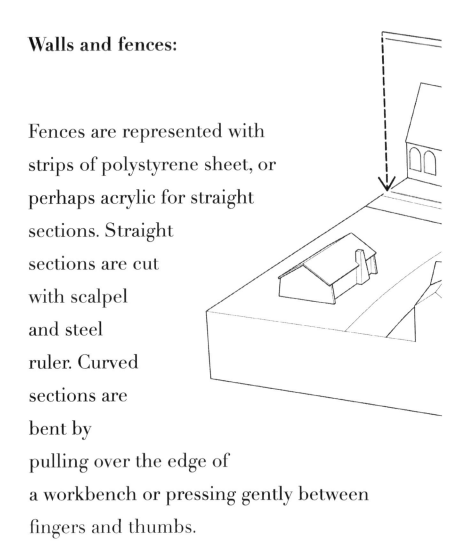

Fences are represented with strips of polystyrene sheet, or perhaps acrylic for straight sections. Straight sections are cut with scalpel and steel ruler. Curved sections are bent by pulling over the edge of a workbench or pressing gently between fingers and thumbs.

The strips are fixed in place with solvent, before painting, or emulsion glue if fitted after.

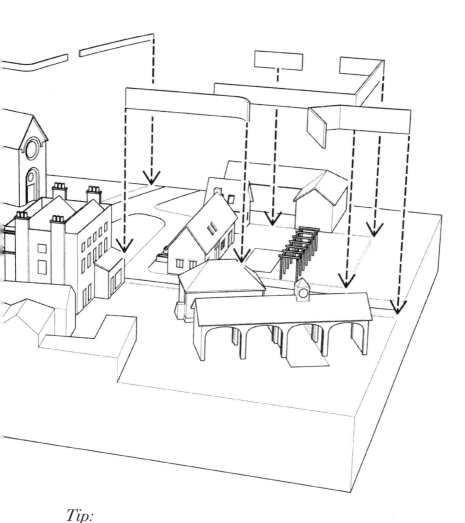

Tip:
Though it may seem appropriate to cut long rectangles, for fencing or other details, with a laser cutter, it will rarely be quicker or more accurate than cutting with a table saw or traditional scalpel and ruler. Unless a great many identical parts are needed, the time taken to create CAD data and set up the machine for cutting will usually make the process longer.

Raised pools:

A raised pool is placed either side of the main entrance to the barn conversion building. These are represented as a 'back painted' clear acrylic block, wrapped with polystyrene strip.

A block of acrylic is cut and sanded to shape, making sure that the sides remain flat and square. Paint is applied to the underside only.

Tip: For painting, clear blocks can be fixed to a board with double-sided tape, face down. The base and sides can be painted, leaving the top clear. The sides can then be sanded to remove paint, ready for gluing.

Polystyrene strips are cut roughly to size, ensuring that one end is cut square. These are glued, with solvent, to the sides of the

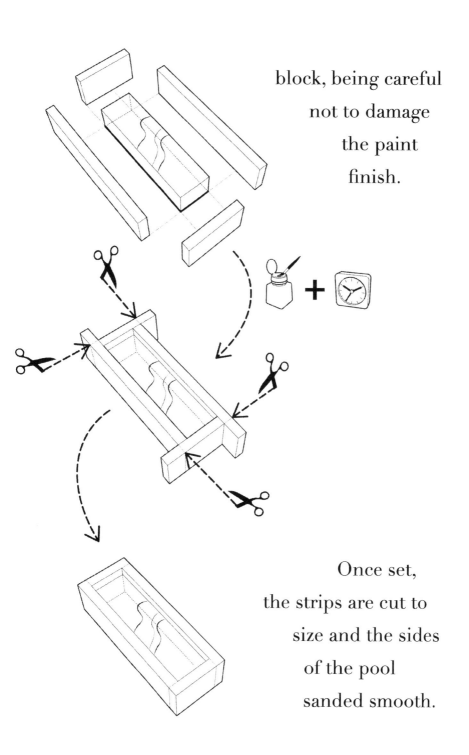

block, being careful not to damage the paint finish.

Once set, the strips are cut to size and the sides of the pool sanded smooth.

The top surface of the 'water' is covered with masking tape before final painting of this sub-assembly. These pools are fixed to the base, with double sided tape or emulsion glue, as part of the final assembly of the model.

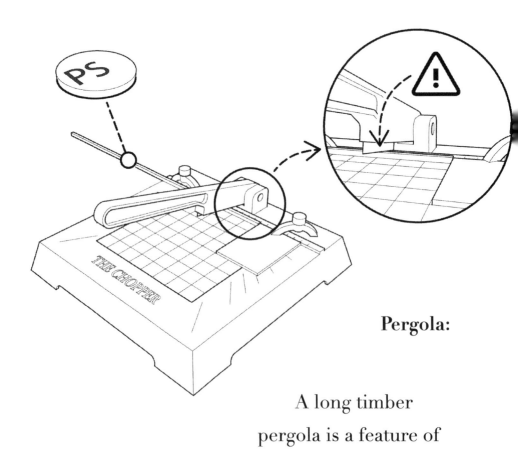

Pergola:

A long timber pergola is a feature of

the 'site'. It is made with preformed square polystyrene strip. This kind of the detail relies on making a number of pieces that are exactly the same length.

Tip: Pre-formed strip is a very easy way to make accurate details for models. It is available in a large range of square, rectangular, round, half-round etc.

A 'Chopper' guillotine tool is used to cut a number of strips that are of consistent length. Pre-formed polystyrene strips are well suited to this kind of detail as they have a consistent section, are easily cut squarely with a 'Chopper' and can be glued easily and quickly with solvent.

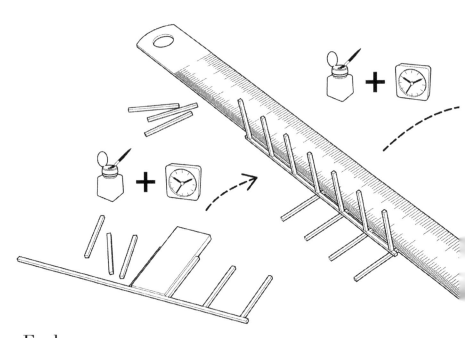

Each side of the pergola is assembled flat using a spacer to ensure that the legs are evenly separated. It is important that these are all the same.

Pieces for the top of the pergola are cut, again with the 'Chopper'.

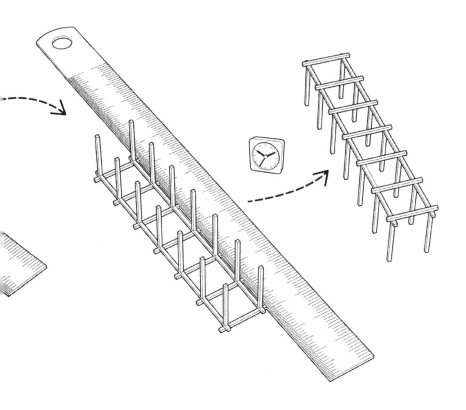

These are
placed against the edge of
a steel ruler to keep them in in line, and one
of the sides glued in place.

Still against the edge of a ruler, the other side is glued in place. Keeping the model against a straight edge during assembly will help to keep it true until enough pieces are fixed to make it rigid. Solvent is allowed to set, so that the pergola can be handled.

The finished pergola is fixed in place with a small amount of emulsion glue at the base of some of the legs. The structure is light enough that glueing every leg is unnecessary.

Tools:

There can be no definitive list of the tools that a professional modelmaker uses. Every model will need a different range of materials, tools and techniques. Often tools are made or modified for a particular job.

A basic list might be...

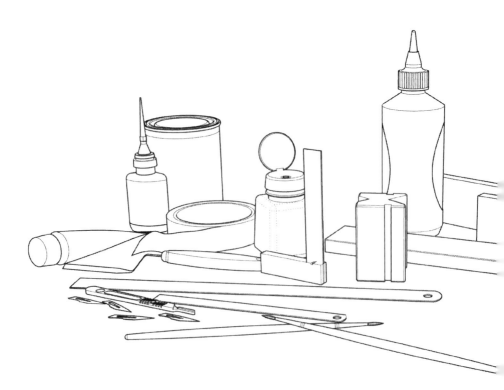

- Scalpel - Swan Morton brand is recommended, its shape making it safer to use than other, round section, brands.

- Scalpel Blades - 10A and 11 sizes are recommended. These should be replaced regularly so that they are always sharp. Use a 'sharps bin' to store used blades.

- Metal Ruler - For both measuring and cutting against. Some thin, flexible kinds are very useful for marking out curves if held on edge and gently bent.

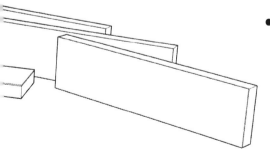

- Vernier calipers - For accurate measuring in many situations.

Sharpening one side of the jaws enables it to also be used for marking out.

- Engineers Squares - For marking and cutting accurate right angles.

- Engineers Square Blocks - A handy alternative to 'ordinary' squares as they are more stable. Often useful as weights too!

- Solvent Pot - For storage and dispensing of solvent. Much safer than a glass bottle as a little solvent can be used at a time without evaporation or the need to remove and replace the lid often.

- Brushes - Small, soft brushes are a clean way to apply solvent when joining plastic. (Not dyed with a strong colour as this can stain the solvent and the model)

- Palette Knife - For mixing and applying polyester filler, cellulose putty and fine surface filler.

- Tape - A selection of masking, double sided and brown parcel tape are very useful for different applications.

- Sanding blocks - Only curved surfaces should be sanded with 'unsupported' paper. All other sanding should be done with hard, flat, sanding blocks to maintain flat surfaces, and crisp corners on the model.

Sanding Blocks:

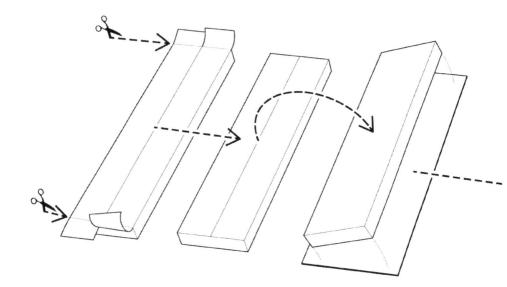

Panels of MDF are cut to the required size (often the width of a sheet of sanding paper).

Double sided tape is stuck to the surface of the block and trimmed to the edges with a scalpel. The backing paper is peeled off and the block stuck down to the back of the paper, ensuring that the paper lies flat.

The paper is trimmed to the edges of the block with a scalpel.

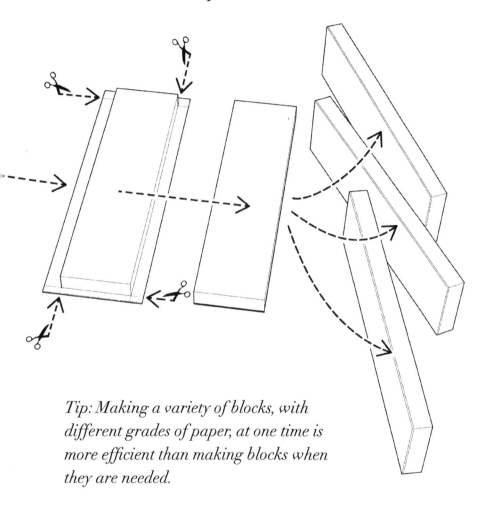

Tip: Making a variety of blocks, with different grades of paper, at one time is more efficient than making blocks when they are needed.

Tip: Double sided sanding blocks can have different grades of paper. One for shaping and one for finishing, both on the same tool.

Medium density fibreboard (M.D.F.):

A manufactured timber board that is available in a range of consistent thicknesses. Easy to source, cut and finish. Can be fixed with traditional PVA wood glue and, if necessary, screws. Its lack of grain and even consistency make it suitable for cutting into both wide panels and thin sections.

A good choice for CNC machining, though not always suitable for laser cutting due to toxic gasses and soot produced when it burns.

Plywood:

A manufactured timber board made with 'plys' of veneer layered and glued together.

Sometimes a lighter weight alternative to MDF for some situations. Often not very suitable for CNC machining as its layers can delaminate and splinter.

Some grades of plywood, often known as 'laser ply' are well suited to laser cutting as they burn cleanly.

Acrylic sheet:

A hard plastic that is available in a range of accurate thicknesses. It cuts and engraves well with a laser cutter. 'High Tolerance' acrylic sheet is recommended for architectural models as the thickness of sheets is more consistent. It can be glued together well with a solvent (dichloromethane / chloroform or similar).

Acrylic sheet is often known by the trade names Perspex, Plexiglass or Lucite.

Cast v Extruded Acrylic:

Cast acrylic should be used in preference to extruded as it will machine more cleanly, due to its higher melting temperature.

Polystyrene (styrene) sheet:

Softer than acrylic and with a melting point too low for laser cutting, styrene is best cut with a knife or scalpel. It can be glued with many of the same solvents, though care should be taken as it will dissolve far easier.

Suitable for pavements as it is easy to cut with a scalpel and thickness is consistent.

Pre-formed polystyrene (Styrene) strips are a convenient alternative to cutting styrene sheet into small sections and strips, for making details and structures.

Textured polystyrene (styrene) sheet:

A range of different textures are available, in different thicknesses that can be used to represent building materials (brick, stone, tile...).

Like smooth polystyrene sheet this can be used unsupported for small panels, but larger pieces should be supported to avoid the soft styrene twisting over time.

Model board:

A 'modern', polyurethane, alternative to timber.

With no grain to be filled and primed, and very even consistency throughout the blocks, a smooth finish is easy to achieve. Blocks can be cut with a table saw and / or band saw, sanded with electric sanding machines and sanding blocks, and finished with all common paints.

P.V.A glue:

Traditional white wood glue. An excellent choice for joining both natural timber or manufactured boards. Sets by drying.

Ideally, materials should be clamped or taped in position, while the glue dries, to avoid risk of moving out of alignment.

Emulsion glue is similar, but slightly more sticky and rubbery in use, and more elastic once set. Very useful to fix small details, figures and trees etc. A good alternative to 'super-glue' for most small details.

Solvent (dichloromethane / chloroform or similar):

A thin, clear, liquid chemical that can dissolve plastics. It is used to soften plastics on each side of a joint, allowing them to be 'welded' together before evaporating to leave a strong joint.

Joints should be set up 'dry'. Capillary action will draw solvent into the joint.

It should be treated carefully in use as it can be harmful. Eye protection is recommended to avoid any risk from splashing.

Contact adhesive:

A thick spreadable adhesive that it well suited to joining and laminating. flat surfaces. Very useful for cladding baseboard carcasses with plastic sheet and layering contours on baseboard tops.

Contact adhesive is applied to each surface to be joined and allowed to dry before bringing them together and applying pressure.

Some brands will contain solvents that can be damaging to polystyrene, causing it to soften or melt.

Cyanoacrylate (super-glue):

A liquid adhesive that sets almost instantly. Only suited to joining non-porous materials.

'Super-glue' should be used very sparingly if assembling finished model parts as it allows no time for repositioning and will leave white or 'frosty' marks. Should never be used near parts of a model that must remain clear. It will leave permanent, matt frosted patches.

Emulsion glue is usually a good alternative for fixing small details.

Polyester (car body) filler:

A polyester paste, designed for car body repairs, that is easy to mix and sets quickly. A small amount of catalyst is added to the filler paste, usually in a ratio of about 5:1 (Golf ball : Pea).

This filler should be used sparingly, applying only what is needed. Once set the filler can be sanded easily to a smooth finish. It is well suited to filling model board as it will set to a very similar consistency.

If metal tools are used they can be cleaned easily by warming them gently with a lighter, or similar, to soften the filler for scraping off.

Over time, as solvents evaporate from the tin during use, the filler may 'dry out'. It can be easily revived with the addition of a little polyester resin (as used for GRP lay up).

A water based fine surface filler can sometimes be an alternative as it can be more easily applied without the need for much sanding.

One part cellulose putty is also useful. Applied to the joins between styrene panels, it can be smoothed by brushing with a little solvent, avoiding sanding altogether.

Notes:

Printed in Great Britain
by Amazon